50 Very Short Conversations

Book One

Copyright©2021 by Mark Kulek

No part of this publication may be reproduced, stored in a retrieval system, or transmitted in any form or by any means, electronic, mechanical, photocopying, recording, scanning, or otherwise, except as permitted under section 107 or 108 of the 1976 United States Copyright Act, without either the prior written permission of the publisher, or authorization through payment.

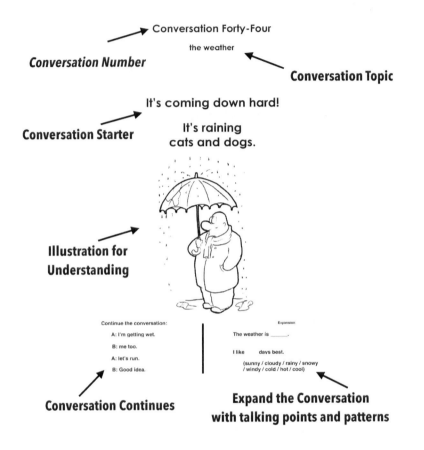

Conversation Number → Conversation Forty-Four

the weather ← **Conversation Topic**

Conversation Starter → It's coming down hard!

It's raining cats and dogs.

Illustration for Understanding →

Continue the conversation:
A: I'm getting wet.
B: me too.
A: let's run.
B: Good idea.

Conversation Continues

Expansion
The weather is _____.
I like _____ days best.
(sunny / cloudy / rainy / snowy / windy / cold / hot / cool)

Expand the Conversation with talking points and patterns

About the Author

Mark Kulek has been teaching English conversation since 1996. He is originally from Los Angeles, California. He now makes his home in Japan where he is an English teacher and a YouTube creator. He graduated from the University of California at Santa Cruz. You can find him on YouTube and at his website - MarkKulek.com

Volume One

This edition starts with conversation one and ends with conversation fifty.

Conversation Themes:

1 & 2 - Greetings	27 & 28 - Invitations
3 & 4 - Around Town	29 & 30 - Making a Mistake
5 & 6 - Asking For Help	31 & 32- Sports
7 & 8 - Asking a Personal Question	33 & 34 - In a Supermarket
9 & 10 - At Home	35 & 36 - Showing Concern
11 & 12 - Being Polite	37 & 38 - Showing Surprise
13 & 14 - Directions	39 & 40 - Displeasure
15 & 16 - Eating	41 & 42 - In My Free Time
17 & 18 - Giving Advice	43 & 44 - The Weather
19 & 20 - Giving a Compliment	45 & 46 - Time
21 & 22 - Imperative Mood	47 & 48 - Happiness
23 & 24 - In a Restaurant	49 & 50 - Saying Good-Bye
25 & 26 - Introductions	

Quizzes

Each conversation has one quiz. There are three possible answers to each quiz, choose the correct answer. Answers to the quizzes are on page 68.

Extension Questions

Each conversation has three extension questions for further discussions.

The extension questions are designed to be engaging and push the conversations to new places of learning.

Watch this book on YouTube

~ 3 ~

Conversation One

greetings

Hello!
How are you today?

I'm good, thanks.

Continue the conversation:

    A: What are you going to do today?
    B: I'm going to the post office.
    A: Bye.
    B: See you.

Expansion:

What are your plans today?

I'm going to ___.

Conversation Two

greetings

Good evening!

Good evening and it's good to see you.

Continue the conversation:

A: What are you doing?

B: I'm just walking.

A: Do you always go for walks?

B: No, just sometimes.

Expansion:

I'm ...ing.

Do you ... ... ?

(always / usually / sometimes / seldom / never)

Conversation Three

around town

I need to stop by the convenience store.

I need to go, too.

Continue the conversation:

    A: What do you need?
    B: I need something to drink.
    A: I need a snack.
    B: Let's go.

Expansion:

Let's stop by _____.

I need _____ from the _____.

Conversation Four

around town

Uh oh - I need gas!

There's a gas station over there.

Continue the conversation:

   A: Over where?

   B: Over there, on the right.

   A: Oh, I see.

   B: Good.

Expansion:

Where? Next to the _____.

There's a _____ (...) the_____.

(by / near / next to / close to)

Conversation Five

asking for help

Excuse me. Does this bus go downtown?

No, it goes uptown.

Continue the conversation:

    A: Do you know which bus goes downtown?

    B: I think it's the B bus.

    A: Thank you.

    B: You're welcome.

Expansion:

Where are you going today?

Maybe, I'm going to ___.

Conversation Six

asking for help

Can you help me with these?

Sure, I can.

Continue the conversation:

    A: That is very nice of you.
    B: It's my pleasure.
    A: Can you possibly give me a ride home?
    B: Where do you live?

Expansion:

Be polite to someone.

Can I ____?

Conversation Seven

asking a personal question

May I ask your age?

Yes, I'm 55.

Continue the conversation:

   A: You look young.
   B: Thanks.
   A: I look old.
   B: No, you don't.

Expansion:

Say no to someone.

Sorry, but _____.

Conversation Eight

asking a personal question

Do you have a boyfriend?

No, I don't.

Continue the conversation:

    A: Would you like to get a cup of coffee?
    B: Sure.
    A: Do you have any preferences?
    B: No, not really.

Expansion:

Practice body language.

You look _____.

Quiz One

1. Hello. How are you (tomorrow, today, yesterday)?

2. Good evening and it's good to (see, saw, seen) you.

3. I need to (walk, stand, stop) by the convenience store.

4. (There, There's, They) a gas station over there.

5. Does this bus (go, goes, do) downtown?

6. Can you (held, help, hold) me with these?

7. May I (say, tell, ask) your age?

8. Do you (have, meet, keep) a boyfriend?

Extension Questions

Conversations 1&2 (greetings)

1. Do you greet people with a smile? If not, why?
2. Are greetings important? Why?
3. Practice other greetings.

Conversations 3&4 (around town)

1. What does convenience mean?
2. Why do we say convenience store?
3. Make a list of items that you can buy there.

Conversations 5&6 (asking for help)

1. Do you help strangers? Why? Why not?
2. When do people need help? Make a list.
3. Practice asking for help.

Conversations 7&8 (asking personal questions)

1. Is it okay to ask personal questions? Why? Why not?
2. Do you mind answering personal questions?
3. Make a list of personal questions.

Conversation Nine

at home

I like to dust.

I like to iron.

Continue the conversation:

A: What else do you like to do?
B: Well, I like to do the laundry.
B: How about you?
A: I like to dry the dishes, but I don't like to wash them.

Expansion:

List some household chores.

I like to _____.

Conversation Ten

at home

Breakfast is ready.

Great! I'm hungry.

Continue the conversation:

    A: Do you want butter for your toast?
    B: Do you have peanut butter?
    A: Yes, I do.
    B: Can I have that?

Expansion:

What do you put on your food?

I put _____ on my _____.

Conversation Eleven

being polite

Please have a seat.

Thank you.

Continue the conversation:

    A: How can I help you?
    B: I need some information.
    A: What is it?
    B: I need to know …

Expansion:

Please have _____.

May I _____?

Conversation Twelve

being polite

Can I pour you something to drink?

That would be nice.

Continue the conversation:

A: What can I get you?

B: Let's see … What do you recommend?

A: Purple Sunrise is a popular drink.

B: Sounds good. I'll have that.

Expansion:

Offer to do something for another person.

Ask someone to do something for you.

Conversation Thirteen

directions

Where is the station?

It's down the street, on your right.

Continue the conversation:

    A: Sorry. Where is it?
    B: It's down the street, on your right.
    A: I got it, thanks.
    B: All right.

Expansion:

Practice echo questions.

Where is ___ ?

Conversation Fourteen

directions

I'm looking for the pool.

The pool is next to the gym.

Continue the conversation:

A: Is the pool heated?

B: Yes, we keep it heated year round.

A: Fantastic.

B: Enjoy the pool.

Expansion:

Ask about things in a hotel.

I'm looking for ____.

Conversation Fifteen

eating

Please pass the salt.

Here you are.

Continue the conversation:

    A: Can you get me a fork?
    B: Here it is.
    A: How about some milk?
    B: Get it yourself.

Expansion:

Practice requests.

    Can you _____ ?

Conversation Sixteen

eating

Eat all of your breakfast.

I will.

Continue the conversation:

   A: Don't forget to wash your plate.

   B: I won't.

   A: After that, brush your teeth.

   B: Don't worry.

Expansion:

Practice imperatives.

Don't forget to ____.

Quiz Number Two

9. I like (to , a, too) iron.

10. Breakfast is (postponed, ready, done).

11. Please have a (chair, sit down, seat).

12. Can I pour you (same thing, something, some) to drink?

13. It's (down, on, in) the street, on (you, my, your) right.

14. I'm looking (on, for, in) the pool.

15. Please (throw, drop, pass) the salt.

16. Eat (all, none, some) of your breakfast.

Extension Questions

Conversations 9&10 (at home)

1 What chores do you do?
2 Do you keep a clean house?
3 Make a list of things you need to do at home.

Conversations 11&12 (being polite)

1 Do you know any impolite people?
2 Are you polite to your family?
3 Practice being polite.

Conversations 13&14 (directions)

1 Have you ever been lost? Please explain.
2 Have you ever given directions to someone? Explain
3 Practice giving directions.

Conversations 15&16 (eating)

1 Do you like vegetables? Which ones and why?
2 What's your favorite meal?
3 How often do you cook?

Conversation Seventeen

giving advice

How can I lose weight?

You should stop eating sugar.

Continue the conversation:

    A: How can I stop eating sugar?
    B: You need to use willpower.
    A: I'm not sure that I have any.
    B: You have to try.

Expansion:

How much willpower do you have?

You should _____.

Conversation Eighteen

giving advice

I've been super tired lately.

You should take vitamins.

Continue the conversation:

    A: How will vitamins help?
    B: They will give you important minerals.
    A: Which ones should I take?
    B: Start with B12.

Expansion:

Talk about pros and cons on vitamins.

How can people improve their stamina?

Conversation Nineteen

giving a compliment

Have you been working out?

Yes, I have.

Continue the conversation:

    A: You look very nice.
    B: Thank you.
    A: Did you get a new haircut?
    B: Yes, I did.

Expansion:

What change would you like to make?

I want to change my _____.

Conversation Twenty

giving a compliment

Yours looks great!

Thanks. Yours does, too.

Continue the conversation:

   A: Not as good as yours.

   B: I wouldn't say that.

   A: It's true.

   B: Thank you very much.

Expansion:

_____ as _____ as _____
(first item + be verb + as + adjective + as + second item)

(Soccer + is + as + fun + as + basketball)

Draw something and then explain what it is.

Conversation Twenty-One

imperative mood

Don't touch that!

What's wrong?

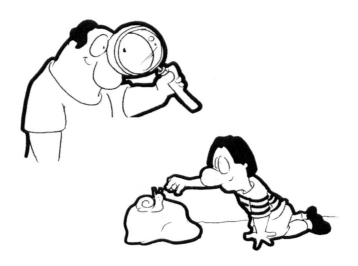

Continue the conversation:

A: It looks dangerous.
B: It's only a snail.
A: I don't like snails.
B: What about escargot?

Expansion:

We shouldn't touch ____.

I don't like ____.
What about ____?

Conversation Twenty-Two

imperative mood

Be quiet.

Sorry. I didn't realize I was noisy.

Continue the conversation:

    A: The baby is a light sleeper.
    B: I hope I didn't wake her.
    A: I don't think that you did.
    B: That's a relief.

Expansion:

Do you know any light sleepers?

  I hope I didn't _____.

Conversation Twenty-Three

in a restaurant

Can I start you off with an appetizer?

Yes, you can.

Continue the conversation:

    A: What can I get you?
    B: I'll have potato skins.
    A: Good choice. Is that all?
    B: Yes, thank you.

Expansion:

What's your favorite restaurant?

It's ____.

Conversation Twenty-four

in a restaurant

Does this seem cold to you?

Yes, send it back.

Continue the conversation:

    C: What's wrong sir / madam ?

    A: My steak is cold.

    C: Sorry. I'll bring you another one.

    A: Thank you.

Expansion:

I like my steak ____.

rare / medium rare / medium / medium well / well done

Quiz Number Three

17. How can I (gain , lose, get) weight?

18. You should (use, eat, take) vitamins.

19. Have you been working (in, out, up)?

20. (You, Yours, Our) looks great!

21. (Don't, Do, Did) touch that!

22. Sorry. I didn't realize I (am, was, will be) noisy.

23. Can I start you (on, out, off) with an appetizer?

24. My steak is (cold, warm, hot).

Extension Questions

Conversations 17&18 (giving advice)

1. Do you like to give advice?
2. What is the best advice you have received?
3. Practice giving advice.

Conversations 19&20 (giving a compliment)

1. Did you give someone a compliment today?
2. Did you receive a compliment today? Explain
3. Practice saying: I like your _____.

Conversations 21&22 (imperative mood)

1. When do you get angry?
2. Are you strict?
3. Practice giving orders.

Conversations 23&24 (in a restaurant)

1. Do you like going out to eat?
2. Explain a bad experience you had in a restaurant.
3. Practice sending food back.

Conversation Twenty-Five

introductions

This is my brother and sister.

It's nice to meet you.

Continue the conversation:

    B: How old are they?
    A: They are 10.
    B: Are they twins?
    A: Yes, they are.

Expansion:

This is my ____.

Draw your family tree.

Conversation Twenty-Six

introductions

May I introduce you to my family?

I would like that.

Continue the conversation:

    A: Everyone, say hello to my friend.
    C: Hello. What's your name?
    B: My name is Karen.
    C: Hello Karen. Welcome to our home.

Expansion:

Brainstorm family activities.

Most families like to _____.

Conversation Twenty-Seven

invitations

Come out with us. You'll feel better.

All right, thanks.

Continue the conversation:

    A: This is a fun restaurant.
    B: It looks really nice.
    A: We come here once a month.
    B: I'd like to come back.

Expansion:

I feel down when _____.

How about _____?

Conversation Twenty-Eight

invitations

Wanna come over?

I can't. I have to study.

Continue the conversation:
- A: Too bad.
- B: I'll be done in a few hours.
- A: Come over when you're finished.
- B: See you in a couple of hours.

Expansion:

Turn down an invitation.

I can't. I have to ____.

Conversation Twenty-Nine

making a mistake

I'm sorry.

That's okay.

Continue the conversation:

    A: I hope I didn't stain your rug.
    B: I don't think you did.
    A: Is it new?
    B: No, it's pretty old.

Expansion:

I'm sorry for _____.

I hope I didn't _____.

Conversation Thirty

making a mistake

Oops, I got it wrong.

Try again.

Continue the conversation:

A: Is this correct?
B: Yes, it is.
A: I don't like making mistakes.
B: It's OK. That's how we learn.

Expansion:

I don't like it when I _____.

I hate when people ___.

Conversation Thirty-One

sports

Can you play baseball?

Yes, I can.

Continue the conversation:

    A: How about badminton?
    B: Sure, I can. How about you?
    A: Yes, I'm pretty good.
    B: We should play sometime.

Expansion:

I can _____.

I can't play _____.

Conversation Thirty-Two

sports

Do you want to go swimming?

No, I'm hurt.

Continue the conversation:

A: What happened?
B: I was playing Frisbee.
A: Frisbee? How did you get hurt?
B: I fell down.

Expansion:

What happened?
I was ____.

What is good sportsmanship?

Quiz Number Four

25. This is (your, my, mine) brother and sister.

26. May I introduce (you, him, its) to my family?

27. Come out with us. You'll (know, feel, do) better.

28. Wanna come (over, in, out)?

29. That's (good, bad, okay).

30. Oops, I (made, get, got) it wrong.

31. Can you (watch, play, go) baseball?

32. Do you want (in, to, play) go swimming?

Extension Questions

Conversations 25&26 (introductions)

1. Tell us about your family.
2. Are you good at remembering names?
3. Practice introducing people.

Conversations 27&28 (invitations)

1. Do you like socializing?
2. Invite someone out for drinks.
3. Make a party invitation.

Conversations 29&30 (making a mistake)

1. Do people learn from mistakes?
2. How do you feel when you make a mistake?
3. Are you forgiving? Please Explain.

Conversations 31&32 (sports)

1. Are you athletic?
2. Would you rather watch or play sports?
3. What's your favorite sport?

Conversation Thirty-Three

in the supermarket

Where's the cheese?

It's on aisle 3.

Continue the conversation:

    A: Thanks. How about yogurt?
    B: It's next to the cheese.
    A: Thank you for your help.
    B: It's my pleasure.

Expansion:

My favorite supermarket is ____.

(Ice cream) is in the (frozen food) section.

Conversation Thirty-Four

in the supermarket

I'm going to the supermarket.

Get some milk.

Continue the conversation:

A: Take a look in the fridge.

B: We need tomatoes.

A: Anything else?

B: No, that should do it.

Expansion:

Get some ____.

Do we need ____?

Conversation Thirty-Five

showing concern

Are you all right?

Maybe.

Continue the conversation:

    A: You don't look so good.
    B: Yeah, I feel a little dizzy.
    A: I'm calling an ambulance.
    B: Thank you.

Expansion:

What happened?

I hurt my _____.

Conversation Thirty-Six

showing concern

Do you want to talk?

Yeah, I do.

Continue the conversation:

    A: What's wrong?

    B: My girlfriend left me.

    A: Oh no! Why did she leave?

    B: She found a new boyfriend.

Expansion:

I lost my _____.

I'm sorry to hear that.

Conversation Thirty-Seven

showing surprise

Did you just rob the bank?

Don't tell anyone.

Continue the conversation:

A: That's not good to do.

B: I know, but I'm broke.

A: You should take it back.

B: But I need it.

Expansion:

It's bad to _____.

Have you ever done something bad?

Conversation Thirty-Eight

showing surprise

Oh my!

Haven't you ever seen an alien before?

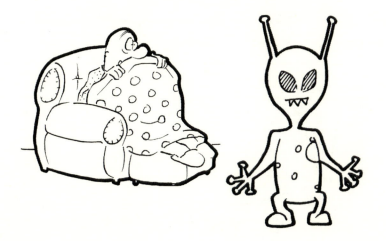

Continue the conversation:

    A: No, I haven't.

    B: Well, here I am.

    A: Where are you from?

    B: I'm from very far away.

Expansion:

Do you believe in aliens?

I don't believe in ____.

Conversation Thirty-Nine

displeasure

You overslept!

What day is it?

Continue the conversation:

    A: It's Monday.

    B: Do I have to work today?

    A: Yes, you do.

    B: I should get up now.

Expansion:

I sometimes ____.

Which is your favorite day of the week?

Conversation Forty

displeasure

Yuck!

It looks rotten.

Continue the conversation:

    A: I don't think I should eat this.

    B: You'd better not.

    A: I can get food poisoning.

    B: For sure.

Expansion:

This ____ is terrible.

You'd better ____.

Quiz Number Five

33. It's (in, on, next to) aisle 3.

34. Get (any, some, a) milk.

35. Are you all (wrong, OK, right)?

36. Do you (need, want, have) to talk?

37. (Do, Did, Want) you just rob the bank?

38. Haven't you ever (saw, see, seen) an alien before?

39. What (date, night, day) is it?

40. It (seems, looks, smells) rotten.

Extension Questions

Conversations 33&34 (the supermarket)

1. Do you like going to the supermarket?
2. What's your favorite section in the supermarket?
3. Make a shopping list.

Conversations 35&36 (showing concern)

1. When do you worry?
2. Are you a good listener?
3. Do you know anyone with depression?

Conversations 37&38 (showing surprise)

1. Do you like horror movies?
2. Have you been to a surprise party before?
3. What's a good surprise vs a bad surprise?

Conversations 39&40 (displeasure)

1. What does displeasure mean to you?
2. Explain a terrible moment you have had.
3. Make a list of things that you don't like.

Conversation Forty-One

in my free time

What have you been doing?

I've been relaxing.

Continue the conversation:

    A: How long are you going to stay there?
    B: It's my day off.
    A: But there's lots to do.
    B: I'll do it later.

Expansion:

What are you doing?

I'm ____.

Conversation Forty-Two

in my free time

Nice shot.

That was perfect.

Continue the conversation:

A: You got lucky.
B: No, it was all skill.
A: Yeah, right.
B: I can do it every time.

Expansion:

In my free time I like to ____.

I enjoy ____.

Conversation Forty-Three

the weather

Summer is the best season.

No way! Winter is the best.

Continue the conversation:

A: I like summer because the day is long.

B: I like winter because I can ski.

A: That's a good point.

B: You have a good point, too.

Expansion:

I like summer because ___.

I like winter because ___.

Conversation Forty-Four

the weather

It's coming down hard!

It's raining cats and dogs.

Continue the conversation:

A: I'm getting wet.

B: me too.

A: let's run.

B: Good idea.

Expansion:

The weather is _____.

I like ____ days best.

(sunny / cloudy / rainy / snowy / windy / cold / hot / cool)

Conversation Forty-Five

time

Got the time?

Yes, it's 12:15.

Continue the conversation:

   A: Thank you.
   B: Why do you need to know the time?
   A: I have an appointment today.
   B: Don't be late.

Expansion:

I usually get up at ____.

I sometimes stay up until ____.

Conversation Forty-Six

time

What time do you want to leave?

7ish.

Continue the conversation:

A: Well, we need to get going.

B: I'm almost ready.

A: Okay - hurry up.

B: Don't worry.

Expansion:

Are you sometimes late?

I'm late because _____.

Conversation Forty-Seven

happiness

I got an A+.

That's terrific!

Continue the conversation:

A: I studied hard for this test.
B: I didn't.
A: Why not?
B: I was busy.

Expansion:

I'm happy when ___.

I'm sad when ___.

Conversation Forty-Eight

happiness

My first tomato.

That's a big one!

Continue the conversation:

A: I'm so happy.

B: It looks delicious.

A: I'm going to make a salad.

B: Can I have some?

Expansion:

I like to ___.

I don't like to ___.

Quiz Number Six

41. What have you been (do, doing, did)?

42. That (is, will, was) perfect.

43. Summer is the (worst, best, last) season.

44. It's raining (a lot, like, many) cats and dogs.

45. (Got, Have, Need) the time?

46. (When, How, What) time do you want to leave?

47. I got (an, a, the) A plus.

48. That's a big (ones, too, one)!

Extension Questions

Conversations 41&42 (free time)

1. What's your favorite free time activity?
2. Do you get two days a week off?
3. Make a free time plan?

Conversations 43&44 (the weather)

1. What's your favorite season?
2. What type of climate do you live in?
3. Practice greetings with a weather topic.

Conversations 45&46 (time)

1. What's your favorite time of the day?
2. Do you wear a wristwatch?
3. Write your schedule for a typical day.

Conversations 47&48 (happiness)

1. Are you a happy person?
2. What makes you smile?
3. Make a list of things that made you happy this week.

Conversation Forty-Nine

saying good-bye

I'm gonna miss you.

I don't wanna go.

Continue the conversation:
- A: I'm going to be lonely.
- B: I'm already sad.
- A: Don't go.
- B: I have to.

Expansion:

I sometimes miss ___.

Do you travel much?

Conversation Fifty

saying good-bye

Good-bye.

Please come back again.

Continue the conversation:

A: I will.

B: I'll be waiting for you.

A: I had a great stay.

B: I'm happy to hear that.

Expansion:

Tell us some of your experiences staying at a hotel?

When you travel, what do you miss most about home?

Extension Questions

Conversations 49&50 (saying good-bye)

1 Are good-byes difficult for you?
2 Have you said good-bye to someone forever?
3 Practice saying good-bye.

Quiz Number Seven

49. I'm gonna (see, know, miss) you.

50. Please (came, come, send) back again.

KeyWords

I'm good.	don't touch	have been
Good evening.	sorry	perfect
I need …	appetizer	No way!
Uh oh.	Send it back.	coming down
Excuse me.	This is …	Got the time?
help	may I introduce	7ish
May I … ?	You'll feel better.	That's terrific!
have	wanna	a big one
like to	That's okay.	miss you
ready	oops	come back
have a seat	Can you … ?	
something	Do you want to … ?	
down / your	where's	
look for	Get some …	
please pass	maybe	
all	want to	
lose weight	anyone	
You should take …	Oh my!	
workout	overslept	
yours		

Quiz Answers

1. today
2. see
3. stop
4. there's
5. go
6. help
7. ask
8. have
9. to
10. ready
11. seat
12. something
13. down / your
14. for
15. pass
16. all
17. lose
18. take
19. out
20. yours
21. don't
22. was
23. off
24. cold
25. my
26. you
27. feel
28. over
29. okay
30. got
31. play
32. to
33. on
34. Some
35. right
36. want
37. did
38. seen
39. day
40. looks
41. doing
42. was
43. best
44. like
45. got
46. what
47. an
48. on
49. miss
50. come

50 Very Short Conversations

Book One

By Mark Kulek

English Conversation Practice

▶ YouTube

🔍 search **Mark Kulek**

Made in United States
North Haven, CT
08 June 2024